Gray Hairs in the Mirror

by

Shane Williams

Dorrance Publishing Co
585 Alpha Drive
Pittsburgh, PA 15238
Visit our website at *www.dorrancebookstore.com*

ISBN: 979-8-8868-3270-9
eISBN: 979-8-8868-3665-3

You wake up one day and look in the mirror. You see a picture of an old face and gray hairs. Are you happy? Are you satisfied? Have you accomplished everything in life? How is your health? You're healthy, you exercise…feel like you could do more, maybe? You've been good to people; maybe you've done a good deed or two. You're a giving person, and you gave and gave; maybe you have more to give.

Look really deep in your mirror; what do you see? Gray hairs really, really show that you may be a foolish person, may be an intelligent person, may be a kindhearted person, and whether or not people are good to you. You're in good spirit because maybe, yes, life has been good to you. You have accomplished everything, was raised properly by two good parents, had a loving caring family, went to school. You had a lot of friends growing up, received your education, you grew up to be that decent man or woman. You feel real good about yourself. You have a good life; maybe you don't have a good life, but you still became an achiever. Did a lot of people look down on you?

What was your class of people? So you never would be influenced by anyone, you've had goals and nothing was going to stand or get in between that. I am nothing. Gray hairs, what are they? Do they mean you're just aging with time, or it doesn't matter, as long as you continue to accomplish everything and prosper, maybe you have different gray hairs.

Maybe your gray hair is the opposite; maybe it shows hardship from a hard life and a not-so-perfect life. Not perfect at all. Maybe that means you're not satisfied. You've done good and people spit in your face. Curse you out, hated you, jealous of you, hated you to the core, hated you and everything connected to you. But you somehow kept a smile on your face and continue to do good, even with a broken heart.

Maybe you are different, more different than you know. A sad person, a person that life dumped on. Didn't get all your education. Maybe you had no friends growing up. Maybe your friends picked on you and beat you up. Maybe you were a high school dropout. Maybe a certain thing was the reason for that. Maybe your prosperity years passed you by. Maybe you feel like there's no hope, although you're a good-hearted person. Maybe you love life. Maybe you don't love life. Maybe you look in the mirror and really hate what you see; your gray hairs make you cry. Maybe you wish you were young again and could do it all over again. But in a different way, somehow, starting with decent surroundings and a good class of people.

Have you ever gotten married, had a family, kids, maybe a pet, dog or cat, big home in the suburbs? Were you a dreamer? Daydreaming; maybe you was just a person on the outside looking on the inside all the time. You look in your mirror, and you feel like you've gotten nowhere. You don't feel lucky or blessed at all, regardless of the good deeds you've done in your life.

Do you go to church? Do you pray? Do you believe in God? Whatever religion you are, do you feel whole and complete? At this time in your life, maybe you've never made thousands a week. Maybe you've worked crummy jobs with minimum wages, could barely make ends meet. Not like the other fortunate people who seem to be doing better than you and have it all. They have big homes and nice cars. You live in a tiny high-rent rundown apartment. Maybe you take transportation, walk or ride a bus.

Your life seems to be much harder than people who maybe don't have a good heart. No, not good like your heart is. Maybe a lot of some people have it easier and don't do good at all. They are evil and might be mean and dump on others or look down on others who don't measure up, or I'm not on their level.

Reader, are you really perfect at what you see in your mirror? Maybe somewhere inside you, there is a dark side of you. Maybe your gray hairs are covering up a bad devil, but when you look in the mirror, you see a saint. A perfect person who can do no wrong. Okay, there are some people who don't know what the words suffering or hardship mean, but there are people that do know that meaning.

Life. It's like Santa Claus; it can have a bag of goodies in it or a bag of crap. Every man's gray hairs show something different. Maybe you're washed up and it's all over, because there's no way anyone can rewind time and do anything over or relive any life that, perhaps, you've missed out on. How do you swallow that?

Okay, so maybe life has been good to you. You lived, you did everything, been everywhere, experienced a lot. You raised a loving family, you have grandkids, a nice big house, have a lot of money in the bank. Now you just want to enjoy your family. That's cool. Keep your gray hair until it turn white as snow, okay? Turn you into a snowman; it's a wonderful life.

When you look in the mirror, unfortunately the world doesn't revolve around you. If a mirror could talk, what would it say to you most? Well done, you're complete. You've done it. Maybe it would say a job well done. So many years have passed and you've seen the sunshine every morning and the moon and stars glow bright every night. Have you accomplished everything? You don't even mind aging and getting more gray hairs, so what more could you possibly wish for?

If you had one wish, what would it be? Now ask a poor struggling person that same question; that person would continuously be wishing. Have you ever looked down on anyone? Even the person standing next to you? Maybe that person is grayer than you. Could that person be more fortunate than you? Maybe, maybe not. Maybe that person is dirty and needs a bath. Is your heart good enough to help that person? Should I call you Mrs. or Mr. Perfect?

Well, the mirror you look in every day can't foresee your future. You can only see how much older and how many gray hairs have developed. Were you born with a silver spoon in your mouth? A poor person trying to act rich? Or was all this the whole makeup for you, period? Maybe the way you are runs in the family. Are you from a goodhearted wealthy family or a conceited wealthy family?

Do people even judge themselves when they look in the mirror? I do. I see myself as one of the hard life struggling people who continuously have to scratch and claw their way up the ladder. Nothing was ever given to me at all. I was raised by a single mother, without a father, but I continued to dream, dream, and dream. People have looked down on me. They move from me. Maybe to them, I didn't measure up to their status or didn't look like a somebody. They made it clear they didn't want to be near a nobody underdog. I've been an underdog. I've been an underdog for as long as I can remember. See, I hate my gray hairs, my life is incomplete, nothing wasn't ever given to me at all in this life.

When I look in the mirror, I see gray hairs attached to a piece of shit, and I have a good heart. People only look at what you are on the outside, not what you are on the inside. But I guess I'm just one of many who feel this way. Maybe you don't. You might feel good about yourself. I understand how some young people feel today. I've been rejected, bullied, and picked on by other kids in my childhood days. I'm surprised I grew up a positive good person and not a negative bad person. I was no trouble to my mother during her time on Earth. Lord, rest her soul, and my grandmother's, and others who have passed in my family. I know they're resting in the bosom of Abraham.

Have you ever cried in life? I have cried many times. It's okay, it just means you're human. No matter how old you get, it's okay to cry and smile if you are happy. Maybe you've been a person that had good luck all your life. Or maybe you're not a real person…maybe you're a fake person who has a face for everybody. Are you two-faced or a back stabber? Are you a liar or a cheater? Are you an honest person? Are you trustworthy? Are you to be trusted? Yes or no?

Do you have any hidden addictions? Are you a drug addict and alcoholic? A sex addict? A gambling addict? A wizard? A leader or a follower? Strong minded; or are you weak minded? When you see your gray hairs in a mirror, how do you describe yourself? Everyone's reflections shows them something different. So maybe you're a thief, a robber, or a a killer. Have you ever had any thoughts of any of these things? Okay, maybe you are perfect; maybe you're not perfect.

Do people see you like you see yourself? Okay, if you knew you were going to die tomorrow, would you accept that? Would that be okay? The fact that maybe your life is fully completed. Okay, you think you would go straight to heaven, and everyone else would go to Hell, right? Are you a self-righteous person?

Regardless of your race, creed, or color, male or female, you have more gray hairs than me. Does it make you better than or vice versa? Hell no, you son of a bitch. You're not better than me, and I'm not better than you. See, we both can die and bleed. Gray hairs are part of aging, although longevity is not guaranteed, but every being in life is hoping and praying for that. To live a long time in this universe, sharing and breathing life with the good and bad people. Every man is a sitting duck. If you wanna live anything, live it quick. No one lives a second time; there's only a one-shot deal at this living thing. Although you made room for it.

Whether you want to be rich, or maybe poor wanna be poor, just do nothing in life, period. Being poor is easy, but making it ain't. So when you look in the mirror and see gray hairs—a whole lot of gray hairs—is that a blessing? Yes…if your life is completed. Wonder if your life is incomplete? Can you ever be happy no matter how many gray hairs you see? Knowing that you can't do anything over, you want to relive it all? No way; you lived already and it's done, whether it's complete or not, that's the deal in life.

Have you ever had fun? Gone to the beach in the summer? Or movies? Or have gone to an amusement park? Anywhere across the world? Maybe you went fishing, jet skiing, or maybe you went sight-seeing in a foreign country, went out to dinner with your spouse. What about any trips? Have you been anywhere? Are you thinking? Think really hard; remember, time is ticking—tick-tock, tick-tock—and time is passing every second, minute, and hour. Think about it. A clock is not our friend. A clock has a lot to do with a human aging and the gray hair process. A clock and a mirror are against mankind; they're our enemies. One passes your time, and the other shows you how much time has passed by. All may not agree, but think really hard and you just may agree.

Living this life sums up to being introduced to your destiny—nothing more. So as people are aging and getting grayer each day, I guess praying, hoping, and dreaming are all we have each day. We can only thrive to do more and more and more and more, but stay positive while you're thriving.

So as I continue to talk about gray hairs in the mirror, my name is Shane Williams (a.k.a.) Photo Prince. I'm a photographer and a writer, but my mission at this time and moment is to continue to talk about this gray hairs in the mirror. I just want everyone to think about what you see when you look in whatever mirror you're looking in. Maybe you're rich, can you get that? Maybe you don't give back. If you're poor, you can't give back, get up and get out so you can give back. How about that? Don't always look for handouts, cuz no one ain't got to give you anything and don't owe you anything. Every man owes themselves. Take it or leave it; that's how the ball rolls for everyone. Do you feel me?

Maybe you have a magic wand or you snap your fingers and make it happen for yourself. Well, I wish I had that same magic. If you have it like that, can you share it with me, please? Because I don't have it like that. This life is a mystery, just like looking in a mirror; you wonder and wonder. Maybe it's wonderful to just wonder; maybe it's not wonderful to wonder. What do you think?

Maybe you go to bars, have a couple of drinks, and talk about how your day went. Do you smoke weed? Do you smoke cigars? Look, I'm not judging anyone. I put my pants on one leg at a time. Are you a hustler? A pimp? Maybe you're a drug dealer? Or maybe you're an angel out of heaven? Are you gay? Straight? Bisexual? Hey, it's your life. What you do behind closed doors is your business.

All anyone has to do is look in the mirror; the mirror will talk to you just like I'm talking to you. So you're not what you wanted to be in life…do you ever wonder what you could've been? Maybe you still have a shot at it. Is time on your side? Do you ever count the gray hairs on your face or your head? It's too many to count. What does each gray hair stand for? Do you stand for something, or do you fall for anything? Think. Please think. Every man's destiny depends upon this. I'm not trying to scare anyone; I just want everyone to use their brains and think when they look in the mirror.

Okay, you see changes from maybe five years ago, ten years ago, maybe fifteen years ago. You see yourself looking more and more different each time you look in the mirror. Maybe now you feel you need makeup, or maybe a total makeover. Do you accept what's going on in your aging process? When you begin looking at your sagging potbelly, flapping arms, do you use your brains and think when you look in the mirror? Do you work out? Do you think now you've gained weight? Maybe you feel you let yourself go. Maybe you don't have time to work out; you're caught up in work and family activities.

Are you married? Have you ever cheated on your wife or husband? If so, not good. That's unfair to both of you. Do you have kids? Do they love and accept you? Are they understanding when they look at you?

Winter, spring, summer, fall, mirror, mirror on the wall. I see a receding hairline. I'm getting bald. Okay, you think you need a wig, a toupee, or maybe you should just shave the rest of it off. What about your teeth? Are they good? Falling out? Okay, maybe you need a pair of false teeth now. Clip-on or dentures or whatever. Do you eat well? Are you a vegetarian? Do you eat fruits and vegetables? Are you a meat eater? Are you eating healthy? As you age, maybe you're on a diet. Are you fat? Are you skinny? Gaining weight goes hand-in-hand with aging. It doesn't matter as long as you accept and love yourself. You gonna live, regardless of what people say…that's what you should do. People gonna talk anyway, whether you're doing right or wrong. Maybe people been talking behind your back for a long time now.

Are you a classy dresser or an ordinary dresser? Maybe you're ordinary like me. Well, you're old now, so it probably doesn't matter. Have you bought big white sneakers? Most old people love big white sneakers; don't ask me why, because I don't know.

Okay, so you woke up one morning, looked in the mirror, and saw too many gray hairs to count on your head and face, and you said, "Wow.

What happened?" Can you look past that because of your accomplishment? Are you a doctor? Did you save someone's life? Or if you're a lawyer, did you help someone beat a case? Are you a fireman, police officer, or judge? Or maybe you're running for mayor or governor? Or are you running for president? Maybe an athlete? Maybe a singer, maybe a rapper, or an actor? Maybe you're a model, a book writer? Hell, have you ever been anything when you were young? Maybe all you've been was a stay-at-home couch potato, sitting at home in front of your TV with a six-pack, eating popcorn, farting, and scratching while your life passed you by? If so, who's the blame? Look in the mirror.

Look at your calendar. Flip the pages as the days and weeks go and go and go and go, nonstop. Time never stops, but life does, at some point. Well, I don't know, maybe you are living. Maybe you have parties night after night, and you have so much money you don't know what to do with it. Do you have a chauffeur? Do you own a motorcycle? Maybe you're an old person trying to act young again. Maybe you don't act your age at all. Maybe you missed out on so much of your young life. Maybe you didn't mature.

The world has been through a lot. The Black Lives Matter protest. I do believe in justice, but peacefully and without destroying things. Also here comes Covid-19. I don't agree with that punishment. Or was it a curse upon men? Who knows? Too many passed away; that's a fact. Did you get vaccinated yet? Have you thought about it? I've gotten both my shots—Moderna plus my flu shot. Everyone's mirror is saying something different, I guess. Question: Does everyone have to continue to get vaccinated forever? The remainder of our lives? Is that in the wild cards for all of mankind future, or is all of this nightmarish thing just a passed-by thing? What does 2022 behold?

Okay, so if the earth was ending tomorrow, would you even care? I mean, the way things have been the last two years. Some probably wouldn't give a damn. Others might care, and others might be undecided or confused about that question. Ask yourself if aging and getting grayer and grayer is worth it, not knowing if the nightmare will continue next time you look in the mirror. Ask yourself that. Which avenue or directions should we all take now as a people? Maybe we should all go run and hide or stand tough with our chest standing out. Take it like a man. Through your many years of living, you've learned a lot of things. Life is a learning experience. Maybe you've learned how to be a better person, a better husband, or a better wife. Maybe a better provider. Maybe you learned how to manage your money a little better. Maybe you've learned how to be a better parent, a better boyfriend or girlfriend. Maybe you've learned how to manage your business, learn how to dance, learn how to drive. Maybe you've even learned how to be a more loving, caring person. I have learned, as well, to be a more of a go-getter, have a better mindset, and stay focused. I stay away from negativity, and try to surround myself with positive people.

When you're old and gray, you're supposed to be a smarter, brighter, wiser, braver, settled-minded, and intelligent, so when every person looks in their mirror, they see a mortal image. There is no man who's immortal; we would all live to be 1000 or 2000 years old, and I know we would hate to see ourselves in the mirror then. Our image would look scary and harsh. Well, I guess we would all just be grateful to still be living, regardless of whether you're one in a wheelchair or on a cane.

So every man just has a limited time on Earth, correct? How do you want to be remembered? Are you planning to leave a legacy behind? Most people with famous careers have left behind a legacy. Most ordinary people can't leave any legacy behind because they're unknown in life, so maybe a person should become known somehow. Okay, maybe you're a private, outgoing person, and you don't want any exposure of your life. That's cool. You're not the only one who may think like that. I will admit, we are living in crazy times today. This day and age, there are a lot of crazy things going on; that's facts, not fiction. There's a lot that no one, including me, understands anymore. I am as puzzled as the next man. But, anyway, we continue to live.

Do you read a lot? Are you adventurous? Maybe you like socializing a lot. Talking, I mean, maybe like teaching others, helping others learn. Maybe you like working on projects for crafting. See, we all have some kind of purpose in this life, as we age and get grayer. Man is on the move. Life is a moment all by itself. As the world turns, as the world turns. However it turns, we must adjust to it no matter how it is. See, our bodies will die, but our spirits will live on forever somewhere, because God said so. Even the people we've lost. Their spirits continue to live on somewhere. Maybe by knowing this, some people aren't worried about aging and turning gray, because aging and getting grayer are the pathway to seeing your loved ones again one day. And maybe that brings a joy because they're waiting for us.

So as you get older and grayer, you talk and walk every day. Maybe go sit in the park every day, feeding the birds. In the fall, you sit and watch the brown leaves drop, and in the winter, you sit in the park and watch the snowflakes drop. In the spring, you sit in the park and just watch the children play and people walking, jogging, and bike riding. In the summer, maybe you sit, reading a book or talking to another aging gray person. These are things that make you feel better about aging. So looking in the mirror every day is now something to look forward to. What is left for an elderly person to do while watching a young woman or man walk by? What? Think about sex? Get her ass? Most old people can't get it up anymore, or they can't remember how it's done. I don't know, maybe some old people do have sexual feelings and can get aroused by whatever sexy scene they see. Who knows. As we continue to age and get older, I bet we will find out, eventually.

Are you a veteran? Have you ever served in the Army? Fight for your country, the United States of America? Or maybe that was one of your dreams when you were younger. You've had many dreams through your life; some came true, and some didn't come true. Maybe none of your dreams ever came true, like so many people.

Looking in the mirror every single day, you see the gray just building, and building, and building on your head and face. It seems like you've been getting older by the minute, second, or maybe hour, and maybe, deep inside your soul, you have this deep burning feeling to add more to your life or just wanna do more. Well, when you start to get old or when you're getting older, people, your body is changing on you, I mean, the way it feels. Maybe your vision isn't as good anymore. Maybe your knee joints aren't as strong as they were before. Maybe now you have arthritis. Maybe your memory isn't so sharp; maybe now you forget a lot of things, Aging has a lot of downs to it. It also has its ups, but mostly downs, because it means your body is beaten and worn, and you have to force yourself to do more every time. Many or some aging folks may agree with me or disagree, but this book is called *Gray Hairs in the Mirror*. I call it as I see it.

Okay, maybe you would like to take a razor and shave your head and face bald. That's okay, but remember, those same gray hairs will be fully grown back in a week or two. You cannot make time disappear. Time is forever, people, and it's been that way since the beginning of time. There is no pausing of time. Time will continue, whether you're dead or alive, and that's a fact.

Let's look at changes. The cost of everything has shot up through the years. Maybe when you were born, things were just a nickel or a dime, and now things cost hundreds of dollars. Your bills are even higher. And forget about stretching a dollar; a dollar ain't gonna cut it. We all need thousands of dollars to make it nowadays. No questions, that's the reality in which we now live. I guess being rich is the only way, at least that's how it seems. You've seen many birthdays, Thanksgivings, and Christmases, and those were blessings and gifts. Seeing holidays is a blessing and a gift. And New Year's; what was, or is, your New Year's resolution? Did it come true? Whatever you wished for, life is the best gift we all have; there is no gift under a Christmas tree better than the gift of life. Maybe there is.

Some days you just want to take something and throw it through your mirror after you look in it, shattering it into many pieces. Please don't bring seven years of bad luck on yourself. Do you believe in bad luck? They say crossing a pole going down the street is bad luck; is it? Maybe bad things only happen if we believe they will and vice versa. With good luck, you believe in good luck. Good things happen for better or worse, so let's all try to think good thoughts. Let's also try to believe in a miracle. If you could count every gray hair on your head and face one by one, how long do you think that would take? Days, months, maybe years? That would be an impossible task.

Okay, so each day you look into the mirror before you start your day. Maybe today you'll go to the mall or go walk on the beach. Maybe going to the library to read some books is a little more relaxing. I hope while you're there, you pick up my book, *Gray Hairs in the Mirror*, and read it. Or read whatever book that interests you. Are you a traveler? Maybe you want to take a trip? An old person can still have fun, right? Maybe go to a state fair, and enjoy a hotdog or lick an ice cream cone. What about cotton cand? Maybe you might go to the art gallery and look at some paintings. Maybe you may enjoy standing watching street performer.

Okay, so you decided to do you now. You stop doing so much for others, because now that you're old, you wanna enjoy all you can enjoy while you still can. While you still have the energy. Maybe you might do some volunteer work; well, if that's what you like doing, then you can't resist helping others, anyway, so do it. How about going to the zoo and seeing some animals? Maybe going fishing? Have you ever dreamt of being an astronaut and going to space? Do you know how to swim? Then go swimming. Please look around for sharks. Do you know how to surf? How about ice skating? Maybe you might go see a basketball, football, or baseball game…that sounds like fun, doesn't it? What about going to the movies? Now that you're old, the littlest things that didn't mean anything when you were young mean so much. Holding tight with your friends and family also means a lot to you now. You just like being around a lot of people; you don't want to be alone. Does being around people comfort you? Maybe make you feel alive? Make you feel strong because you can draw strength from others just by being around them?

Okay, so you're just trying to find the best way to cope with aging. You've paid your taxes all your life. You've contributed all your life. You've tried to be the best you could be all your life. Regardless of your race, have you ever faced racism? Well, I know I have. If you're black, that goes without saying. But for any race or culture, is each gray hair you can count an experience? Or a couple of gray hairs? Maybe you can even tell when your gray hairs first started growing, or maybe you didn't pay any attention to it until later in your life. Each day you woke up and saw the sun shining in your bedroom, you just opened your shades or blinds to brighten your house. Maybe you've seen a rainbow after a rainy day once or twice, and it gave you a good feeling on which path or direction to take in your future. Every person has to make those choices very carefully, because the path you take in life could make you successful or a failure.

My name is Shane Williams. I was born in November of 1972; I'm a Sagittarius. In 1985 at age 13, I wrote rap rhymes, although I never became a rapper. I guess that's where my writing talents came from. I picked up freelance photography in 1998. Remember the days of the black and color roll films? Wow! Well, that's when my photography talents began. Although I had talents, I still worked crappy jobs like security, messenger, and a parking attendant. I decided to take better, higher steps. I even tried modeling; I guess I was too short and not so good looking. I've auditioned for actor's rep. I don't even know if that agency is still around…that was 1996 in NYC. Well, see, I'm not successful; I've lived an ordinary life. I face struggles, clawing and trying to make it. Yes, I've been to many food pantries. I've even been on public assistance. I'm one of those whose life was not so good; my gray hairs show hardship and struggles. I could never laugh or throw my head up at anyone in those shoes, because I know what it's about.

People who look in a mirror and see scars of struggles and hardships are warriors. They can conquer anything. You can't go any further down then you already are. Those people with silver spoons in their mouth could never understand that I never wanted to be a goodie-two-shoes type of person. Yes, there were people who thought they were better than me who moved from me because maybe they dressed better or had more education. Today, as a long and gray-haired bearded man, I carry a lion fur of courage and determination blowing behind my head. It is a forceful shield of armor against jealous and hateful doers who may hate me. You hate me and may not like me; that means I have something special. Anyone who faces what I faced, this is you, too. It's not easy being stepped on like a roach, but you accept it, make the best of it, and let it make you a soldier. All people from all walks of life are blending down here on Earth.

Okay, maybe what makes you a warrior is that you're a cancer survivor. Maybe you beat breast or prostate cancer, or maybe you overcame some other illness. Okay, you are a warrior, too. See, not just going through hardships makes you a warrior. Many obstacles in life could make your skin tough like a crocodile's leather skin.

Are you a maker and a taker? What I mean is that you make real money the honest way, right? Well, I put my pants on one leg at a time. I wouldn't have wanted it any other way. The sweat of your brow, that's real labor. I feel making money the hard way is the real way. Your parents might have earned money the hard way, and you might have earned money the hard way. So why not introduce that same labor method to your kids? Let your kids understand that making money the hard way creates a strong-minded hard worker. Let hard work show on your hands. It shows on mine.

As you look in the mirror and see your gray hairs, have you seen justice in this world? For any race, cops are justified killing another race. White on black crime is justified. That's what all the protests on black crime are about. Black-on-black crime, rappers killing rappers. Most people are acquitted in courts because of their correct skin color. The young will not see their gray hairs in the mirror if this injustice continues. Do you ever sit down and wonder what the hell is going on in this world? Why is this happening? What's the reason these things are happening? There's right and wrong in this world; you can either believe in the right, or you can believe in the wrong. Does skin color matter? Maybe, maybe not. Does skin color have a lot to do with what kind of job position you get? Maybe how much money you make? How about where you live? How about whether or not you get convicted when you commit a crime? Maybe some people are the right skin color, and others are the wrong skin color?

Have you ever voted? Maybe, maybe not. Maybe that would've made a difference in this world. As you look in the mirror and see age in your gray hairs, do you ever wish you had voted? If you have never voted, no matter where you lived, you had many mayors, governors, and senators, and we've all had many presidents. Have you seen any changes for the better in this world from when you were young, until now, when you're old? Yes or no? Maybe, maybe not. Or are things still the same as they've always been? Or maybe you've seen just a little change so far? There's a whole lot more, and a ways to go, before things might, you might say, get better.

Do you wish you had gotten involved in politics? A democrat or republican? Maybe it takes one to believe and trust one in order to become one. Have these politicians and leaders through the years been for all of us or some of us? Everyone in the world is supposed to be united, because this is the United States of America, right? Are these divisions created because of certain matters and issues, as people agree or disagree, approve or disapprove, come together or apart? Feeling different and thinking different is not a crime, right? No one can feel or think the same, right? A man's brain is completely different from the next person's. They look different, they walk different, and talk different. Man on earth is plain different. Male and female is different, night and day are different, the sun and moon are different, nothing or nobody is the same. Old and young is different. The picture IDs in your wallet are different. Your debit and credit cards are different. Looking in your mirror every morning proves that.

Is life about wisdom or making money? Or both? If life is just about money, that kind of sucks. That means people are walking around rich with money in their pockets but with empty heads. People should have money, but I think life should be based on knowledge, wisdom, and education. So all the young people out there who desire a lot of education, stay in school, stay in college. Grab it because knowledge is power.

It's more difficult for women to look in the mirror every day, seeing facial changes week by week and year by year. Age, which comes with gray hairs, is one definite thing you see. You're middle-aged or past middle age. Do women accept their changes better than men accept their changes? Well, most women make a crazy remark seeing just the littlest change in their appearance, even though they're surrounded by people who say they look wonderful. Okay, what about when she looks in a full-body mirror and might see the slightest weight gain? Oh my goodness, the roof might fall in, cuz some women flip out that smaller clothes don't fit no more and maybe she may also think her best years are behind her, or whatever. If you had kids, well, you should have expected the weight gain, because that's part of it. Measurement size, or much bigger, that's okay. You might even be a grandmother. Well, let me tell you, I like more pushing for the cushion! Let me tell you how good you look.

Do you still have a sex life in your middle or old age? You freak, you! Okay, good, that's keeping you feeling young, right? And less tension, and relieves stress, right? Okay. Men's perspective of aging is in gray hairs.

Are you married? Do you ever tell your wife how good she still looks after all these years? Remember, you're aging too. Is she letting you know how good you look, as well? I think that's part of loving each other. Couples embrace each other…I mean, I guess you're supposed to, from an aging man's perspective. Give a man a magazine and a private restroom space, and that might be all some men ask for. A private place to think. Yes, the restroom.

This life can be funny, happy, and sad. It can sometimes make you mad. Whether you're doing good or bad, be glad to look in your mirror and see your gray hairs. You're becoming an old hag, and that's not so bad. Check out my rhyming skills. Life can be like a beautiful rainbow or sunset, or the most beautiful painting you've ever seen. Or it can be so heartbreaking, like tears in a puddle. As we walk in day-by-day or step-by-step, or talk word after word, we are already just living in a dark room, feeling our way through life. Simple-minded people can't foresee a damn thing. As we continue to look in the mirror, can we not see that our shadow is protecting us? Or is it just that they're following us to show us our darker side? Every man has a bright side of him and a dark side of him; does that mean maybe we all are born in this world with good and evil inside us or a part of us? Maybe so.

Do you dream of maybe relaxing someplace? A dream that makes you feel real nice, like a glass of red wine. Maybe a shower with lots of money flowing over your whole body, or maybe you dream about being a mermaid, swimming in nice, clear ocean water? Do you dream about being a prince, king, or princess? Well, even your pets dream. So as an old person, maybe you really, really cherish your memories. You have pictures hanging on your wall—very old items you might have collected through the years—and you're not throwing anything away, regardless of what anyone says. Treasured memories. An old person guards those memories because they help you remember the most wonderful times in your life, from your day of birth to a child, a teenager, a grown man or a woman, and, yes, an old grandma may also have the same treasured records. Video of the family, joyful times, albums and books that had collected dust. Everything is dusty. Maybe old shoes have good memories. Also, old clothes are a memory. Hats, scarf, maybe a pair of gloves with holes in them; everything that you kept in a box or in your closet has some kind of meaning, and therefore, you made it a part of you. You now treat each memory as if it was fragile, and it must be protected. I agree you should protect your memories, young and old people.

So you wake up each day, look in the mirror, and you ask yourself, "Well, what should I do today? Do something in the community? Help other old people? Maybe sit and talk and possibly learn something else new? Maybe someone might learn something from me. Maybe I get a slice of pizza. Maybe I might go to McDonald's or a nice Italian restaurant and see what's on the menu. Through your years of experience, you have done so many things, been so many places, seen so many sides. Maybe you've been married several times. Maybe you've been divorced many times. Also weather. You're an old man or woman, either way there are young people who would love to hear your years of experience. Maybe you don't wish to tell all of your experiences, but now, in your old life, everything seems to mean so much to you. Every heartbeat, every breath, every blink, every step, every laugh, every tear, every cheer, every happiness. Maybe you even pick up pennies off the ground. Maybe you may even pet a stray cat or a stray dog.

You value life now more than ever. It's just important to you. So you exercise, right? Eat right? Live right? Do good for evil, right? Pray right? Help others the best you can, right? Keep a clean mind and heart, right? Keep love in your heart and not hatred, right? Accept others as they are, right? Love your wife or husband the way they are, right? Love your kids and grandkids, even if you may not agree everything they do is right? Don't let no sickness or health condition get the best of you, right? As you continue to get older, aging and with gray hair, continue to let the gray hair show, right? Be proud that you lived to get old, right? Also be proud to have a receding hairline, right? Let your wrinkles continue to show without any makeup, right? Keep on limping with your cane, right? Walking with your walker? Keep on wheelchairing your wheelchair, right? Keep your spirit up with a smile on your face, right? Continue to show the young folks what you can do, right? Continue to show people how smart you are, even though your memory isn't so good anymore, right?

Do you think now that this everyday life seems to be getting a little scary? We are constantly wearing facemasks, getting viruses, and we are continuously developing one behind the next and behind the next. First it was plain coronavirus, which, sadly, killed so many. Then delta variant. I also heard about alpha variant. Now omicron, which doesn't seem to be so fatal but very much more contagious. How many shots do we have to get? The first Moderna or Pfizer vaccine shots were thirty days apart, then here goes the second shot. Now here comes the third booster shot several months later. So everyone, main question is how long is this going to continue? Will there be a fourth, fifth, sixth, seventh booster shot? Maybe this is our new way of life. Maybe this is all that everyone's future holds now, before the end of time. We don't even know what's in the vaccine. All we know is that it's supposed to help and protect us, and keep us alive from the viruses. One thing for sure is there's nowhere to run and hide, because even if there was, these viruses will find us anyway, no matter where we are. Well...are these viruses smarter than us people? Maybe, because we cannot outrun it. So as this nightmare continues, and we all continue to look in the mirror at ourselves and age, and gray hairs continue to grow, do we see any end to this nightmare that the world seems to be trapped in right now? With all these viruses coming aboard from out of nowhere, is every man paying for their sins, whatever that sin may be? Maybe God is just mad at the world, or maybe we are feeling his wrath. Maybe God is trying to get all of our attention and is telling us something. Maybe what we all are going through now is a warning.

You think this is a spiritual thing or a natural thing? Who really knows? Americans and people overseas are suffering from the same plague. It's interfering with living and life itself, right? It seems to be blocking us like a severe defense, which has and can continue to decrease lifespan. So I guess people need to pray now more than ever before, and we have to have faith and keep our fingers crossed for the better, and maybe all of this might just one day go away. Stay in courage, keep awareness, keep the faith, stay strong, stand tall, keep your head up, listen, learn focus, stay safe, don't give up, keep moving, keep hoping, keep praying, stay sharp, keep smiling. Crying is okay sometimes too. Sing a good song. As we continue this roller coaster ride of panic and despair, our thoughts and feelings of it all seem breathtaking, like being underwater.

Don't you sometimes feel like cursing and punching a wall because you may be so mad how things have been going since 2020? Although the sun will shine again, everyone can only wonder when and where, and how soon. Is it somewhere over the rainbow? I must say, as I look in the mirror every day and see myself aging and with gray hair, this turned out to be a hell of a journey. Life has a whole new meaning and definition. People now can only see it as far as the ball can be thrown. So are there any more unexpected surprises coming besides all these viruses? Maybe frogs and locus. Maybe the end of time is next for 2022…not trying to scare anyone. Well, we have all lived long enough to know now that anything is possible—good or bad. Okay, everyone seems to be walking upside down; our feet's no longer touching the ground anymore. We are all barely keeping our heads above water, 'cause this world and everywhere seem to be in some deep shit, right? Now let's keep swimming until we see the shore. Then, and only then, we can say we've got out or made it out of all that deep shit. I know it's tough for anyone to smile and really be happy as things once were. May be a while for it again; let's hope it will be again. That's all we can do because, if this is a plague the world is suffering from, I'm sorry to say, our hands are too short and small to box with a higher power. Yes I understand it's like a bad dream; we can't seem to wake up. Just continue to social distance, wash your hands, and wear your facemask.

Just like Dorothy said, there's no place like home. Home seems the only place nowadays to be in. The most time to spend it, being around your family. You have a large or small family? Family shares these fears, laughter, tears, happiness, and sadness with each other. You can find strength being around your family. You all gain power through love for each other, and that helps with keeping your spirits up in this walk of life.

There are so many beautiful people putting their heads together, trying to keep the world safe. EMT workers, doctors, nurses, fireman, policemen. Scientists, because they invent new vaccines that you and I hate to be injected with. So who do we trust? What we see? What we hear? Can we even trust our own family? Or should we trust our family? Only our family? Maybe everyone should be like cave people, because people just only trust who's in your cave, not no other caves. Can we even trust ourself to do the right thing? Maybe some can trust their own self.

Well I was born in 1972. Black disco, black hustling pimp music, and movies. I didn't have much growing up. Yes, I grew up in poverty. I guess I was a little light-skin, fair-looking black child, but I still experience being bullied, and the jealous kids beat me up a lot. Most of the time, I wore the same clothes and kids in school had name brand clothes and sneakers. I was just grateful to have something to wear. So you can see how humble I was. Kids picked at that I had a pair of Vikes, and they had a pair of Nikes. Remember when Nikes came out early 80s? I couldn't afford a pair, but boy, I sure wish I had a pair at that time. That would've been cool. I had a single mom; she didn't have much money, but she did have one thing: she always walked with God. My grandmother also walked with God. I'm grateful to say they both was spiritual. I never knew a father, so I'm not going to write on that. Me and my Aunt Shalaunda grow up together and played together, and most of the time, she would confront kids who beat me up. Well, I would tell her they were bothering me. Boy, she really set them straight; those kids never mess with me again. Now as far as a family or family support, I can't talk much about this topic. The family I had, cousins and other family members, were scattered all over different states.

While family I had, family support I didn't have. I used to wish I had love and support from a family. I guess that's when I became an underdog. Last in line, outside, looking in most of my life growing up. I guess I was also rejected by family. I never sat down and said to myself, "Why me?" I just dealt with whatever bad situation I was in.

Well, like I mentioned in my early writings, I became a writer at age thirteen. The writing started in 1985. Anyway, so I started high school in 1987. Clara Barton High School. It was a vocational school. Well, the only thing I can say about that was that's when I got a lot of girls liking and loving me, and even some of these girls was my secret admirer. They was writing me a letter left and right. Well, that was the ninth grade. I only did two years in that high school because things went downhill after those two years. Remember the word family support that was non-existent to me. I transferred from Clara Barton High School in Brooklyn, New York, to Sara Jay Hale. Then I ended up transferring to another high school by the time I was twenty and one-half years old. Time caught up to my age, or my age went faster than time. My mother's supported me on whatever little she had was hardly anything, but she did her best without a husband. It's not easy for a mother to raise a kid or kids all by herself. So the eleventh grade was as far as I could go before I dropped out, and college, oh, don't make me laugh. Since I was unable to finish high school, well, you just know college wasn't in the cards at all. Whoever had family support and still have family support, don't take that for granted, please don't!

My dear mother, RIP, in and out of mental institutions, suffering from mental disease or just plain stress in life itself. Maybe my mother was a little scared of life. Well, life do have a lot of fears, but I guess you can't let it get you down. My grandmother, RIP, in heaven, she was a no-nonsense type of spiritual person—very solid.

She was also a pastor. My mother and grandmother both were solid, on their feet, Christians. Did I mention this in my earlier writings? No, I don't think so.

My life was like an old dusty car that no one wants to drive sitting in a garage. Anyway, I'm still an underdog until this very day. If I ever have kids, or if I had kids, I would just tell them I love you and do your best. You don't have to be the best. Stay positive, be around positive people, and do what makes you happy. Be happy for you, not me. So as I look in the mirror and I'm aging, with gray hair and face, I don't have a whole lot of education, but I have a lot of common sense. A whole lot of street knowledge. I know that I may down talk myself a lot, but it takes doing that to be a better person. Those, including me, who have always been last in line, you'll be first in line one day, don't worry about that. Those who've always been first in line, you will be last in line one day, you better believe that.

Okay, it's never too late to do anything. Get an education or get married, whatever, just don't have kids too up in age, because the child might be born with some kind of birth defect. Although parenthood might be amazing, think about the child and the suffering it might endure. Well, getting married when you're old is embarrassing, some may say, because marriage is really for when you're young, but you don't have to listen to me; this is just my opinion and maybe others' opinions. Do what makes you happy. I don't think marriage is in the cards for me. Maybe, maybe not. Who knows?

I have osteoarthrosis in both feet, arthritis in both knees, and torn medial and lateral meniscus. Oh, did I mention aging is like a bully? Also, aging can and will beat you up and beat you down, year after year after year, and guess what, people, we can't do a damn thing about it. Aging is a legit bully and legal bully. Aging is the biggest bully of them all. You really won't know the real definition of the word 'bully' until you begin the aging and start seeing all those gray hairs pop up from out of nowhere.

Each time you and I look in the mirror, we see more and more gray hairs growing on your beard, mustache, out of your nose, out of your ears. Those gray hairs are a sign of you and I becoming a Scrooge. And old dirt bag. Laugh if you wish, this cool. Also we're becoming dusty, rusty, and musky old people who have an old smell. Well, I mean, at least some of them. I'm not at that point yet. Well, if I do smell, oh well, what the hell?

When birds chirping, they're singing. When squirrels chase nuts, they're dancing. When bumblebee is buzzing on beautiful flowers, they're romancing. When a man introduce himself to a woman, he's taking his chances. Like the fresh scent, it smells of spring air. The wind slightly below, and as an angel flying in the air, all around our heads, like sunrays shining. You begin to develop hair bumps and relax. Pleasant feeling overcomes your soul and spirit. Inside you're feeling a little peaceful. You get calm. You begin to imagine yourself in a happy dream; you keep your eyes closed as you just jump and dance in the air, as if you had wings like eagles. You're feeling free, with no cares, like a newborn baby. Like a young, innocent child, you spin around and around on fresh green grass. You spin as fast as you can, everything is up in the air. You're laughing real loud. "I'm free, I'm free, I'm free." So we spin around, all around, upside down, like a leaf floating in the air in the fall. Seems like the angels are spinning with us, turning around as they're singing a song of joy. We're up in the air. Keep your eyes closed. We have no more cares. No job, no worries. Spin, smile, and laugh as loud as you can. No more bills, no more viruses, no more vaccine injecting, just love and sound all in the air. The biggest, happiest flow we've ever felt. Keep it going. And as you're singing and are out in the air, rejoicing, all your family is jumping in floating in the air. Your friends. It's love everywhere in the air. We we we, yeah yeah, ha ha, oh ohhhhhhh yaaaaaaa, everybody feel freeeeeee. Close your eyes every now and then. Just imagine a special place in your mind that keeps you feeling free, happy, peaceful, and floating in the air like one of the angels., while other angels are playing the harp in your mind.

Scream as loud as you can. It's a scream of relief. Nothing can bother you anymore or get you down anymore. The pleasant sound you created is your own personal happy ID code. Whatever you do, just don't stop with your imaginary inner peace, floating in the air. Everyone can do this. Everyone should do this; it might help us heal inside our minds and hearts. The world has suffered so much so far. Let what I said be all of our place of retreat. So remember, when we start to feel down and with no sense of direction, just close our eyes, and let's all go to our imaginary peaceful place in our minds to regain that inner peace

Once upon a time, when there was no virus, no vaccine, injection, no eviction, and no joblessness. There was no hungriness, no homelessness, no long Covid-19-testing lines everywhere, on every corner, street, and avenue. No one thought this was how the future was going to turn out and be so far. So, people, is this Hell on Earth? Being in detention right now would be better than this, do you agree with me? Maybe you do, maybe you don't. Well that is, at least, how I feel. Some may say living is unbelievable right now. Some may say it's miserable right now, or even devastating, or the hardest thing that they ever had to face or deal with right now. It's at a point where you just wanna take both hands and pull your hair out. Maybe even pound your head against the wall. I'm not saying harm yourself, but all that's going on, right? The last two years have gotten the best of some people. They've drained them of energy. Or is it also a mental drainage, and it's piled up on everyone? Everyone seems to be buried in despair and hopelessness right now.

It's January 2022. Well, they say a new year is like a new start, a new beginning. I want us all to come out of this as survivors. Let take it step-by-step. Small steps. One step at a time. He says, she says, they said this, they said that. Listen to what sounds right. I know that I'm only gonna listen to what sounds right, because I don't want no regrets down the road. None of us should want any regrets. Listen to what sounds right, not what don't sound right. Always follow what you feel is the right way. Also tell your children the same thing. We must now walk with wisdom and not stupidity, because how you are describes what kind of person you are. Let's do whatever it takes to expand our lives. That's the only way to see age and gray hairs in the mirror.

The way of life is now different, and we must learn how to adjust to it, one way or another. It's like a card game, and we've been dealt a bad hand. Now that being said, I guess everyone must upgrade your face mask. I say just double them up, period. I mean, if you feel like you must upgrade, get the KF94 or N95. Man, things seem like it is continuing to get more and more complicated each and every day. Like Marvin Gaye once said, "What's going on?" Good question. What is going on? I think that song should be played every day, everywhere across the world.

Life and living is the only thing that really matters. Not money, although that is another survival tool. Education, cars, houses, any material thing seems less important nowadays. So should everyone go back to being prisoners of our own homes like 2020 was? remember the streets like an empty ghost town, do you even remember those times repeating itself? Oh God no please.

Governors, mayors, town leaders, everyone talks about what's going on in the natural should. We also look at things from a spiritual base. Could we be in or near the last days, the end of time? The Bible did talk about the last days in earthly plagues, in the coronavirus pandemic could be one of them. Jesus said, "Nation will rise against nation, and kingdom against kingdom. There will be great earthquakes, and in various places, famines and plagues, and there will be dreadful portents and great signs from heaven." Book of revelation. They're not my words, but Jesus and his father, the Almighty God. So we're in a maze. Places to run, many directions and turns, but there are no exits. There are no small or big words in any dictionary that can describe the time we're living in now, but remember and believe what Jesus said. A man has been around for thousands of years. He's the overseer; I'm just a book writer.

How many mirrors do you have in your house or apartment? Well, I know everyone has a mirror inside their bathroom and bedroom. Are there any other parts of your home where you have a mirror? Maybe on the living room wall, or behind a closet door? Okay, do you look in the mirror often? Maybe or maybe not. People who are good-looking stay in the mirror. I guess those people will live in the mirror if they could. People that's not so good-looking could care less, you might say, about looking in the mirror or even having a mirror. I guess they just own one or two mirrors. That's the most mirrors and I'm-not-so-good-looking person owns in their home. And when they look in it and see aging and gray hairs, they probably can accept that more so than when a good-looking person look in the mirror. Well, I'm not so good looking myself. The way you look on the outside as far as beauty shouldn't matter. Only if you're really stuck on yourself, and you can't help it.

After a stressful day of hard work, you just run nice hot water and body wash in your tub, because you need a nice bubble bath. That's where you are when you're able to think and really relax. Some may even go straight to sleep in these tubs, because they may be just plain exhausted. Oh, yeah, the water is soothing, nice, hot, feels like a body therapy. Oh, yeah, you had a very, very hard day, now it's time to close your eyes, lay back, and forget it all. Maybe afterwards you might play some soft music turned down low. You just feel like putting your feet up. Oh, yes, it's just you, and it's your time now. You have on your housecoat, and you're totally in relaxed mode, even mentally. Nothing can get you mad or bother you right now. You've blocked everything out. You're all the way calm now. Are you feeling a feeling of peace? Peace, I said. Maybe you might go in your kitchen and grab some ice cream, maybe a banana split. Maybe next you might go back to your living room, play a movie, or just watch a little TV. Oh, you're doing you, right? Nobody but you. Or maybe you might grab your laptop and do some networking. Maybe you might grab the phone and call an old friend you haven't spoken to in a while. Or maybe you may grab and read your favorite book. Or maybe you'll cuddle with your dog or cat if you have a pet. Maybe you have a diary you may want to continue writing in. It's your quiet time; you may do whatever you want to do to refocus your mind. Yes, quiet time helps refocus your mind, your thoughts, your feelings, and how you may feel about certain things. Yes, quiet time can rebuild everything about you as a person if you want to. Good luck.

Do anyone have any goals? Or set goals in place? Well, any goals come with a sacrifice. My goal is to lose some weight somehow. I am 330 pounds. Well, I was never this size. Well, during the 2020 pandemic, the only thing that was open was a line at a supermarket, and I became hungry each time I passed by a supermarket, seeing that long line to get in. I guess monkey see, monkey do, knowing that gaining weight, it's just as easy to gain than to lose. I was 260 pounds when my mother passed in 2014, so I have no one to blame. The pandemic was part of the blame, but I should have resist temptation. Instead, I was weak like a newborn baby's knees and soft like melted butter. Gyms burn how many calories? If people are still going to gyms, it's remotely. They made gyms at home. Okay, so as I look in the mirror, I see myself aging and with gray hairs. I also see a teddy bear. Well I would like to start to lose at least thirty pounds at a time by slowing down my eating and changing my diet. I work out a little more, and I'm eating healthy, including fruits and vegetables. Junk food is really what put those pounds on. Weight is not good; it causes heart problems and high blood pressure. Well, I already have high blood pressure. It causes diabetes, joint problems, breathing conditions…all kinds of conditions. I know that there's other people out there trying to figure out how to get those pounds off. Well, let's all do it together. Let's work at it or continue to work at it. Instead of eating three meals a day, let's eat one meal a day. Only if you can tolerate that, because nowadays, I can.

I am like a sailor sailing on the rough seas. I'm just going in the directions the wind blows me. I don't have a crystal ball. No one does. I can only see as far as my own hand in front of my face. I cannot see past that, and I am not going to try and see past that. The old saying, "the door swings both ways," well, all we can do with whatever swings in our direction is try to deal with it the best way we can or know how. Life is fragile, as people are fragile. Yes, we can be broken one way or another. We are not made out of robot materials; none of us is the terminator or terminators. Out of all of our knowledge and education, we're still just lightweight, like a bag of cotton. Here today, gone tomorrow, like we never existed. Some may try to leave a mark in life. Jesus Christ is the only man who's ever left a mark in this world. He died on the cross for our sins and then went to Hell. Took the keys to Hell and death then came back in three days. Now that's leaving a mark to see. Man really don't owe another man; we only owe Jesus Christ everything. We're like puppets on a string. We cannot do no more than Jesus allows us to do, because all our life and this world is in his hands.

Remember this, my friends, my readers, my supporters, my haters, followers, my thinkers, educators, big money makers, the role is this life apply to everyone, so get off your high horse every now and then. Come visit down to my level sometimes. I'm ordinary, yes. I am a writer, so what I am is a plain down to earth human. I don't like it at the bottom, but I like staying grounded. I don't have a chauffeur, I don't have a maid, and if I did have a maid, I would probably ask her to marry me. I've been in one or two relationships, both toilet bound. Both got flushed down and wasn't worth one damn brown penny. Used in abused. I'm now protecting my feelings by every means necessary; man and women must protect their feelings. I guess we live and learn.

As I continue this topic—gray hairs in the mirror—I want to also talk about policing all across fifty-two cities and states, because we all need our police departments for protection, right? Recent killings across fifty-two states have led to protesting and riots as people have seen. I seen this also on the news. CNN, ABC, CBS, NBC, and all across all television programs. The officers which supposed to be protecting the community is also killing people in the community they supposed to be protecting. Let's begin with NYC NYPD police departments. There are good police officers, and there are bad police officers, not just in NY, but also in other states. It's unfortunate that you cannot tell the good police officers from the bad police officers; they are good friends with each other. A good one may have a bad partner, both partners might be bad, or both might be good partners. But how would we, as the public, know the good ones from the bad ones? When people need help, I call the police. They really don't know if they will get help from these officers or get killed. No one knows. Police officers, deputies, state troopers…no matter who you are, the community don't know if you're their friend or enemy. They just don't trust the police anymore. There has been corruption in some departments. Let me tell you something law officer in every community the criminals and killer watch the news so when you're a police officer., everyone is going to know what you and your department is doing also the media. If you're a good police officer, ok, good, continue. If you're a bad police officer, you don't need a badge. Your good fellow officers, should turn you in and put handcuffs on your but. A bad officer has no business inside or near a police precinct, unless they're under arrest. The same goes for a deputy and state trooper. Therefore, there seems to be a gap between the police and communities. There is no more trust. It's up to the police in every state to wedge the gap of trust together. You must find a way. Maybe the police in the community need to meet and hold a meeting just between the people in the officers, and just ask the people how can they begin to restore trust back in the communities. It's bad to see good officers get killed, but that's the past corruption's backlash mark. Bad and good officers shouldn't mix, but they do. There's good and evil people who walk, work, and live around each other every day, but what can you do? You have to know the difference, the good from the bad people. Different lifestyles should hint you on that. Bad people, or keeping bad company, can cause nothing but troubles for good people. We must learn from our mistakes and downfalls. Maybe you don't have any mistakes or downfalls, okay. Then those who have mistakes and downfalls: you must learn from that, cuz that life will somehow make you learn from it.

Everything I've written about has been my personal opinions. Maybe some agree, maybe some might not agree. I believe that this world don't have enough love in it among people. Maybe there is no love at all; I don't know. Love can possibly soothe the savage beast. People is supposed to return the same amount of love that you're showing them. And there are some people the only thing that they know how to return back is hate. Young juveniles across America. This word, hate, is all they know. These are lost kids. That's the reason they're carrying guns, hurting people, because they never knew a right path to take. They only know of a wrong path, so that's what they choose. Maybe if they were given a chance to take the right path, well, who knows. Believe me when I say I don't justify no crime. Regardless what race or color, how young or how old, if you do a crime, whether robbing, raping, killing, or stealing, you need to be caught and prosecuted to the fullest of the law. And I guess that's the only if you get caught, or if someone notices you and rats you out. A snitch, of course, and there's hardly no snitches around. Believe that because there's only hard-core true-to-the-street-game people out there. Dropping dime is not popular anymore. It really takes real good souls that's tired of the nonsense to see something, say something mentality. Most people believe in minding their own business, and others are just plain scared to say anything. I don't blame them, but sometimes saying something saves lives or a lot of lives. You must lead by example…is that the old saying? But I'm sorry, everyone is not walking in the same positive path as you and I. Why? I guess that's another unsolved mystery. Well, honestly, this is my first book, *Gray Hairs in the Mirror*. Although I've been writing for years, I just wanted to talk to the people and express my feelings and opinions on certain topics. I'm not writing my first book for fame or fortune, because I'm a plain ordinary person. Today I'm still going to be that same plain ordinary person…tomorrow.

Okay, sometimes I don't shave. Sometimes I wear the same clothes. Yes, I take showers and stay clean, but I'm not changing myself to satisfy anyone. Take me or leave me, that's real and I am being for real. I don't have a lot of anything like other people, but I'm happy and grateful for what I do have. It ain't much, but it's all I have, and it's mine. I don't want what anyone has, I just want what's mine and belongs to me.

As I look in my mirror this morning and see my age and gray hairs in the mirror, ladies and gentlemen, my readers, I finally come to the end of my first book, *Gray Hairs in the Mirror*. My book is based on the reality of life, the way it is and how it is, whether my readers agree or disagree. Believe me, I would love to polish up life like a pretty picture, but life is not always a pretty picture, so I write it as I see and live it. Always love yourself first before you can say you love others. Loving yourself is where it starts. Yes, continue loving those that hate you, and continue to do good to those that spit in your face. Also continue to love your backstabbers, and love those who are jealous of you and don't want you to prosper. We all must continue to be good inside and out. I know to some that's not easy. keep love in your heart, regardless. And no matter what, I thank you all and I love you all, and I hope my readers can begin to love me. Thank you.

Now in 2022

Both black and white people who have gray hairs have lived through years of war, poverty, increased food prices, increased gas prices at the pumps, rent hikes, and are now living through getting shot and killed because their skin is black. Because they might look different. Things must change, people. You look in your mirror and see aging, wrinkles, bags under your eyes, gray hairs, and when you smile, maybe you have no front teeth, maybe you wear braces…whatever you see in the mirror when you're looking at yourself. So to everyone, just love yourself.

Until next time, bye-bye and stay safe, please. Safe from Covid-19 and also the craziness in the world.

And to my loved ones who I wish were still here to see my first book: my grandmother, Thelma; my mother, Delores; Pete; my cousin Judy; Aunt Joyce; and others who have passed on. Also, Uncle Robert, who just passed this year, 2022. Continue to rest in God's peace!